Creating Messages That Motivate

Creating Messages That Motivate

*How to Use and Master
The Decker Grid System*®

Just Write Books • Los Angeles

Published by Just Write Books
JustWriteNow.com

Printed in the United States

ISBN: 0-9749830-4-7

Cover design by Ramona Dsouza, RamonaWorks.com
Layout and production by Joyce Sarkisian

*The Decker Grid System is a registered trademark of
Decker Communications, Inc.*

CREATING MESSAGES THAT MOTIVATE

In this climate of high-velocity change, often you can't get the results you want alone. Instead, you need to inspire those around you to do what's necessary to make the impossible a reality. Because of this, your personal and professional success is determined largely by what you say and how you say it.

Spoken communication is the most effective way to move from ideas to action, and from action to results. It offers a potential that few people use to their full advantage.

This user's manual will help you improve what you say. It will teach you a system that ensures the messages you convey to others will get results. It will change the way you communicate. It will make you a more powerful person.

We call our secret weapon **The Decker Grid System**®—a quick, efficient way to create messages that motivate. It was originally developed more than twenty years ago to help participants in the first Decker communication skill-building programs prepare their spoken messages more quickly and effectively. Since then, more than 200,000 people have been positively affected by The Decker Grid System.

The Decker Grid System is a rigid-sounding name for what is, in fact, quite a flexible and creative process. It is a guaranteed method for developing action-oriented messages that focus on the listener.

What begins as a conscious tool becomes a way of thinking. This system uses several ideas you may already know and puts them together in a new way. Once you learn and then use this system for creating messages, you will:

- Dramatically reduce the time you take to decide what to say
- Avoid dumping data on unreceptive listeners
- Increase listener attention and retention of your information
- Speak confidently at a moment's notice
- Substantially improve your ability to move people to take your desired action

Whether you're leaving a voicemail message, making a presentation to a prospective client, reporting at the next staff meeting, or having a one-on-one over coffee, you will dramatically increase your ability to engage the people around you to help you achieve your desired results. Think of this system as software for the mightiest computer: your mind.

Designed to give you the essentials for creating messages that motivate, this success guide's sections build upon one another. Please read it through the first time from start to finish. After that, keep it as a handy reference and go directly to the section that covers the step where you need help. Contact me if you have questions or comments.

Bert Decker, April 2005
San Francisco, California

Contents

WHAT'S USUALLY MISSING

When we speak with others, we often fail to include one or more of the key ingredients for success. Knowing what these ingredients are will help you understand the power of The Decker Grid System, as it simply and systematically ensures these ingredients are present in every message you communicate.

1

MISSING INGREDIENT #1

The power of the emotional connection. When you speak, you have the opportunity to communicate your emotion along with your information. Your emotional connection will move your message into the hearts of your listeners. It will bring life to the concepts you communicate.

Somewhere along the line, we learned that it's not okay to convey emotion in business. Perhaps we take emotion to mean "emotional" and conjure up images of people weeping or throwing tantrums. Nonsense! Emotion energizes and enables people to achieve greatness. Communicate your conviction! Develop a clear point of view (POV).

PEOPLE BUY ON EMOTION

AND JUSTIFY WITH FACT.

MISSING INGREDIENT #2

What it means to the other person. When you speak, people listen through their own filters. Your key to success is to make certain the message you deliver is so relevant to your listeners' interests that you successfully capture and maintain their attention. It is easy to miss out by becoming internally focused as you prepare to communicate about something that is important to you. Beware, and always strive to reflect the listeners' perspective.

Soon, you'll uncover some easy ways to gain the listeners' perspective. Understanding your listeners is absolutely essential to the success of your message.

MISSING INGREDIENT #3

Netting it out. Like you, your listeners are on information overload. They often wonder how they're going to be able to manage the sheer mass of data that surrounds them. Give them the gift of brevity and include only the essentials. Help them out. Net it out. They will thank you by listening to you, rather than the person who leaves five-minute voicemail messages. Keeping it simple and keeping it brief are just two of the wonders of The Decker Grid System.

NO MAN
PLEASES BY
SILENCE;
MANY PLEASE
BY SPEAKING
BRIEFLY.   —AUSONIUS

MISSING INGREDIENT #4

Telling them what to do. If the purpose of speaking is to influence others, then to be successful, you must tell listeners what actions you want them to take. Sound obvious? Think back to the number of times you have been the listener and have found yourself wondering, *Yes, now what?* Don't leave it to others to interpret your intentions. S-p-e-l-l it out.

Vision without action is merely a dream.

Action without vision just passes the time.

Vision with action can change the world.
—Joel Arthur Baker

MISSING INGREDIENT #5

The all-important WIIFM. That is, "What's in it for me?" The number one way to motivate listeners to take action is to tell them how they will benefit. If you can't think of any benefits, think harder. There needs to be some sort of personal gain for your listeners if you hope to strike a responsive chord.

What's in it for me?

MISSING INGREDIENT #6

Making it two-way. When communication between people is only one-way, it is not as effective as an interactive exchange. The best way to build commitment in your listeners is to engage them in the process. Build in opportunities for dialogue. Ask questions, genuinely listen, and acknowledge their answers.

The Decker Grid System provides the flexibility for two-way communication throughout the delivery of your message.

Knowing the importance of these missing ingredients sets the stage for introducing The New Decker Grid System. Before we launch into the process, let's first cover some basics . . .

FIRST, SOME BASICS...

Choose the right medium for your message. If the spoken and written word had the same effect, you could get everything you wanted in life from writing a good memo. Clearly, speaking and writing are different.

While writing can be detailed, logical, and organized, speaking effectively requires spontaneity and a willingness to interact with your audience. Do not approach these two methods of communicating the same way or use them for the same purposes.

The written medium is best used to inform.
When you have a lot of facts and information to transfer to others, put it in writing. People can read five times faster than you can speak. Writing often activates rational thinking, the logical part of our minds. This is one of the reasons why it's so ineffective to read text when you're giving a speech. Speaking is more than a mere transfer of data.

When you **want to persuade—to move people to action and to reach them emotionally—speak to them.** This guidebook is designed to assist you with persuasive speaking, which allows you to address people in a way that they can "listen" with many of their senses. Listeners are affected by the emotion you convey, your tone and nuance, gestures and volume, and hundreds of other stimuli unavailable in the written word.

With The Decker Grid System, you will never again have to write out a speech, word by laborious word. You will never again drone on and on in a three-minute voicemail message. Your input at a meeting will be heard and, at the very least, considered for action.

In fact, with this system, you won't write *any* sentences to prepare for speaking. Instead, you'll make notes of powerful *trigger words*.

Use trigger words. When you prepare a spoken mess age, don't write out sentences. It is far more efficient to create with building blocks, each one referring to the con-cepts and ideas you wish to communicate. These building blocks, or trigger words, serve as a prompt to the wealth of working knowledge within your mind. You can think of them as file names or key words within files.

Trigger Words: **The shortest word, group of words, or symbols about which you could talk for thirty seconds to five minutes.**

Weight Loss

The following are trigger words to quickly jog the author's mind for a speech about running. Note that they are short and might make sense only to the author. Seeing each word "triggers" more information related to that word.

Trigger words enable you to quickly and easily capture and organize large quantities of information.

Trigger Word Examples for Running

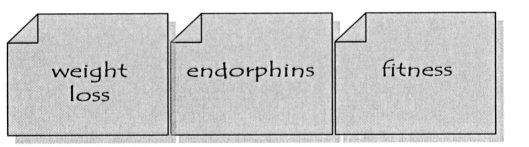

| weight loss | endorphins | fitness |

Fitness

Endorphins

Assemble your tools. The Decker Grid System consists of:

- Message Folders
- Post-it Notes
- This Book

> **Give us the tools, and we will finish the job.**
> **—Winston Churchill**

THE DECKER GRID SYSTEM MESSAGE FOLDERS

The Message Folder is a preprinted tool for helping you brainstorm then organize your thoughts, and then acts as a reference to keep you fresh and on point while you're speaking. These folders are enormously useful for walking you through the five steps of:

1. Laying the Cornerstones
2. Creating ideas
3. Clustering ideas into themes
4. Composing a message that motivates
5. Communicating your completed message

The inside of a Message Folder is shown on pages 14 and 15. The last page of this guide provides information on how you can purchase folders.

The left of the Message Folder assists you with the first three steps. The fourth step, Compose, uses the right page. Your completed Message Folder can serve as a handy reference when you actually communicate your message to your listener(s). It can then be filed and kept for future communications on the same subject.

POST-IT NOTES

Post-it Notes are the great 3M invention of little pads of paper with a strip of adhesive on each piece. Post-it Notes are the means by which you organize your ideas in The Decker Grid System. Your trigger words conveniently fit onto small Post-it Notes (1½ by 2 inches), which, in turn, fit into the squares on the Message Folder.

Post-it Notes are made to be mobile. Not every idea that occurs to you will be used, and the ones you do use could end up in any order. The mobility of Post-it Notes allows you to shuffle ideas around quickly, sorting and discarding them until you've arranged them for maximum clarity and impact. The Decker Grid System prompts you through this activity so that, in no time flat, you achieve order from chaos.

Use them upside down. We have found that Post-it Notes work best in this exercise if you position them with the adhesive at the bottom before you write. This enables the note to curl toward you, making the trigger words easier to read.

USER'S MANUAL

This user's manual for The Decker Grid System is designed to walk you through the process step by step. We encourage you to read it thoroughly the first time and then use it as a reference while you become more adept at using the system.

The Preparation Triangle

Subject:

POV

How YOU feel
about the subject

Use a verb.
Answer the
question,
"So what?"

Listeners

How THEY feel
about YOU and
your subject

Action

What THEY should
do about it

Benefits

What's in it
For THEM

The Presentation Grid

| SHARP | POV | ACTION | BENEFIT |

Main Body

Key Point 1	Sub Point 1	Sub Point 2	Sub Point 3
Key Point 2	Sub Point 1	Sub Point 2	Sub Point 3
Key Point 3	Sub Point 1	Sub Point 2	Sub Point 3

Closing

| POV | ACTION | BENEFIT | SHARP |

CREATING MESSAGES THAT MOTIVATE IS A FIVE-STEP PROCESS

Each step of The New Decker Grid System builds upon the one preceding it.

1 When you lay your Cornerstones, you create the context for your message. The Cornerstones establish the purpose, or foundation. They stimulate your thinking and focus your attention on your listener's perspective, what you want your listener to do, and how he/she will benefit.

2 When you Create, you unleash your mind's potential to generate ideas to support your subject.

3 When you Cluster, you naturally group your ideas according to common themes.

4 When you Compose, you organize and edit your clusters. The end result is your best ideas, arranged and ready to be communicated.

5 When you Communicate your completed message, you have your Message Folder for quick reference, helping you be brief and persuasive.

THE SKILL TO DO COMES FROM DOING

To experience the many benefits of this marvelous system, you need to begin to internalize the first four steps. Commit now to practice each step as you read each section and review the example provided.

TO DO: Think of a communication situation coming up in the next few days. It should be a situation where you will be talking with others to inspire them to do something. It could be a subject at your next staff meeting, a discussion with your spouse about vacation plans, or a favor you need to ask from a friend. Use this situation to practice each of the steps in the process. Do this, and by the time you reach the end of this success guide, you will have developed your message to motivate your listeners to action. The work you do now will dramatically increase your effectiveness. It's guaranteed!

You'll begin by laying the Cornerstones . . .

STEP 1

Lay the Cornerstones for Success. What are you going to talk about? Write your subject in the form of a trigger word or two on a Post-it Note. Open your Message Folder and place this Post-it Note on the upper center of the left page in the cloud labeled Subject. Note that the cloud is rounded with no hard corners. This symbolizes the problem with most subjects: They are too vague with no boundaries to give context and focus to your ideas. The four Cornerstones are designed to solve that problem by providing the context for your communication about your subject.

You'll read an example to illustrate how this happens.

Summarize the subject. Let's imagine I live in a small city of 60,000 people. Recently, this quaint community has grown rapidly. In fact, the population has increased 20 percent in the last three years. I like to ride my bike and run in the parks. I've begun to notice a lot of trash in the parks and on the city streets. This was never a problem in previous years. I've decided to approach the city council with a proposal to begin to clean up our city.

The subject of my message summarized in trigger words would be . . .

SUBJECT

Your Point of View (POV) is your emotional connection to your subject. It brings the ideas you communicate to life.

Determine your POV. Capture the feeling, attitude, or opinion you have about your subject in a few trigger words and write them on a Post-it Note. Put it in the middle of the POV square (upper left side of the Message Folder). To make sure it meets the definition of POV, ask yourself these questions:

- **How do I really feel about my subject?**
- **Why am I going to speak about this subject?**
- **In my opinion, what is the current state of affairs regarding my subject?**

Your POV should reflect your attitude about the subject. It should remain consistent, regardless of the listener, and create a sense of commitment of personal stake. Remember:

PEOPLE BUY ON EMOTION AND JUSTIFY WITH FACT.

EXAMPLE:

To continue our scenario, I would summarize my feeling, attitude, or opinion in my mind: *I feel a formal Clean Up Day is essential to cleaning up our city. It will help get trash off the streets and raise the community's awareness about the importance of a clean community throughout the entire year.* Then I'd make my trigger-word Post-it Note:

POINT OF VIEW (POV)

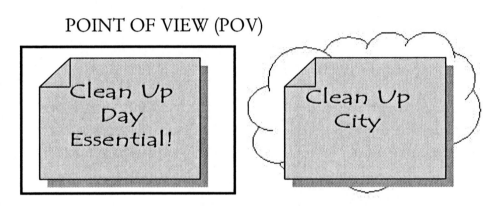

SUBJECT

KEYS TO REMEMBER

- Your POV answers the "so what?" for your listeners.
- It gets you in touch with how you feel regarding your subject.
- Ultimately, your goal should be to have your listeners walk away sharing your POV on your subject.

SECOND CORNERSTONE: LISTENERS

Walk a mile in their shoes. Successful communicators demonstrate an understanding of their listeners. Spend some time thinking about your subject from your listeners' perspective. Generate information in each of these three areas:

- Demographics (age, occupation, responsibility)
- Needs and interests including current knowledge of your subject
- Attitudes regarding you, your organization, your subject, and your POV

You need to be clear about who your listeners are, so spend time identifying their DNA. Just as DNA represents the genetic makeup of a person, so too, DNA in the listener profile identifies the makeup or characteristics of your listeners.

Make your information specific. Write trigger words to summarize your listeners' DNA on Post-it Notes. Place them in the lower left box in your Message Folder. It is absolutely essential to think about your listeners before you begin to create your message. Communication from their perspective will enable you to be relevant. It will keep their attention and help move them to action.

If you don't know much about your listeners, take the time to find out what you can. Call a few in advance, and talk to other people who know them.

P.S. Once you begin to identify your listeners, you may find you have several diverse groups within your large audience. If so, identify ways to address each of their needs or concerns in one message or deliver a tailored message to each group separately.

EXAMPLE:

Some of what I know about council members comes from direct, personal contact and some from what I hear from others. Also, the local newspaper has given me some understanding of the council and its goals. Here's what I know:

The council is made up of our mayor and council members.

Demographics:	• All are long-term residents (> 5 years) • Ages range from 35 to 60 • 60 percent men/40 percent women
Needs & interests:	• They want to improve the town by increasing business and furthering the sense of community. • They have a desire to make some permanent contributions to our city's success.
Attitudes:	• At least two of the members are pro-environment and actively promote recycling.

All of this gets encapsulated, again, into trigger words on Post-it Notes. Turn to page 24 to see how this looks.

KEYS TO REMEMBER
- Focus on your listeners.
- If you don't know much about your listeners, take the time to find out more. Understand their DNA.
- Check in with listeners during your communication to ensure your information is accurate.

The Preparation Triangle

Subject:

EXAMPLE:

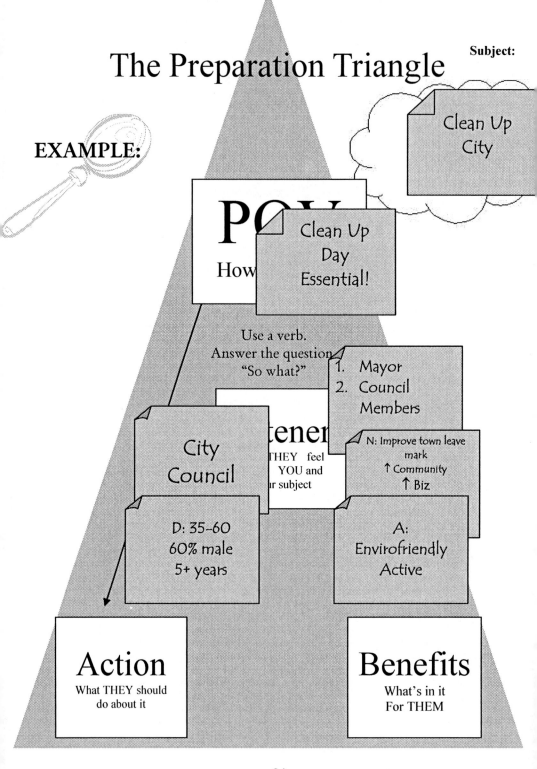

Clean Up City

POV

How

Clean Up Day Essential!

Use a verb.
Answer the question
"So what?"

1. Mayor
2. Council Members

tener

City Council

THEY feel
YOU and
ur subject

N: Improve town leave mark
↑ Community
↑ Biz

D: 35–60
60% male
5+ years

A:
Envirofriendly
Active

Action
What THEY should
do about it

Benefits
What's in it
For THEM

24

Decide what you want your listeners to do after they hear your message. In the process of communicating to them, help them understand where you want to go with your idea. By being clear and specific with your Action Steps, you are telling them how they can further their own interests and meet their own needs.

Choose a General Action and Specific Actions. Write each of them on a Post-it Note and place them in the lower right square on the Message Folder.

The General Action is the **"big" action** that reflects what you would like your audience to do, or feel, or perhaps even be, in broad terms. The Specific Actions should be measurable, realistic, and timebound. Clearly defined Specific Actions will give your listeners ways to demonstrate their empathy or agreement with your **POV**.

By determining Action Steps before you create your message, you will **focus** your mind on your desired outcomes and the resulting message will reflect them.

EXAMPLE:

General Action: I would like the city council to consider the merits of my proposal. I would like them to take these Specific Actions:
- Dedicate the first Saturday in June as "Clean Up Day."
- Promote the event prior to June and actively participate in it.

GENERAL ACTION   SPECIFIC ACTIONS

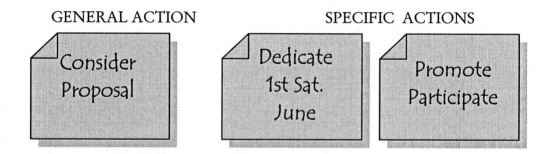

Consider Proposal

Dedicate 1st Sat. June

Promote Participate

KEYS TO REMEMBER
General Action guidelines:
- Be general.
- Describe the big action you want listeners to take, such as being open, considering the possibility . . .

Specific Action guidelines:
- Be specific.
- Make it measurable.
- Be realistic.
- Set a time frame.

The Preparation Triangle

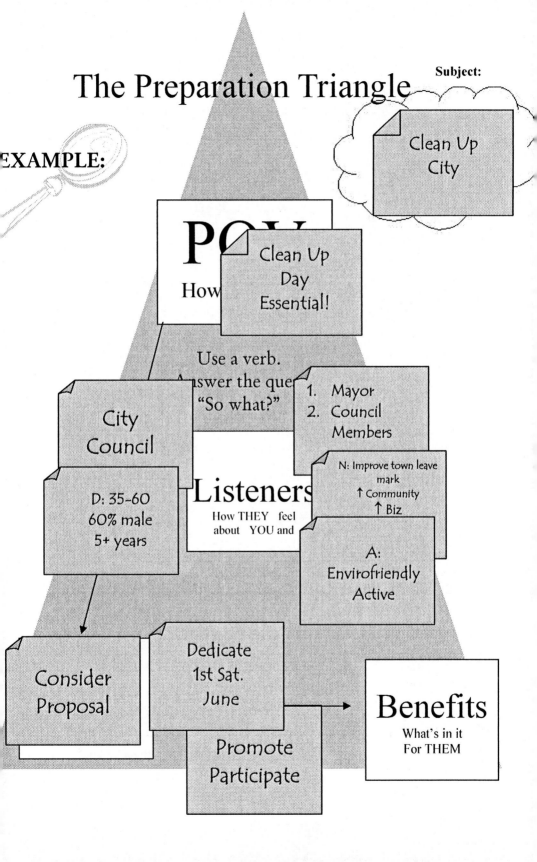

EXAMPLE:

Subject:

Clean Up City

POV

How

Clean Up Day Essential!

Use a verb.
Answer the question "So what?"

City Council

1. Mayor
2. Council Members

D: 35-60
60% male
5+ years

Listeners

How THEY feel about YOU and

N: Improve town leave mark
↑ Community
↑ Biz

A: Envirofriendly Active

Consider Proposal

Dedicate 1st Sat. June

Benefits

What's in it For THEM

Promote Participate

FOURTH CORNERSTONE: BENEFITS

Help them see WIIFM. ("What's in it for me?")
Identify what personal benefits your listeners will receive
from taking your Action Steps. If each listener is agree-
able to your POV and taking those actions, how will he
or she be better off?

Avoid generic business benefits. Identify three benefits that
satisfy the needs and interests of your listeners. To help you
generate ideas, re-read your trigger words in your Action Step
and Listener Cornerstones.

Write trigger words for each benefit on separate Post-it Notes.
Place the benefit Post-it Notes in the box in the upper right
corner of the Message Folder, putting them in order of importance.

EXAMPLE:

If the city council considers my proposal, dedicates the first Saturday in June as Clean Up Day, promotes it, and participates, it will realize the following benefits:

- Citizen appreciation
- A cleaner city
- A permanent contribution to the city's future success

I believe these benefits will be important to my city council based on what I know about them as described by my Listener Cornerstone.

KEYS TO REMEMBER
- Benefits must be specific to your listeners, based on their needs and interests.
- Benefits will result from taking your suggested actions.
- Avoid generic benefits whenever possible.

Have I reached the party to whom I'm speaking?
—Lily Tomlin as "Ernestine"

The Preparation Triangle

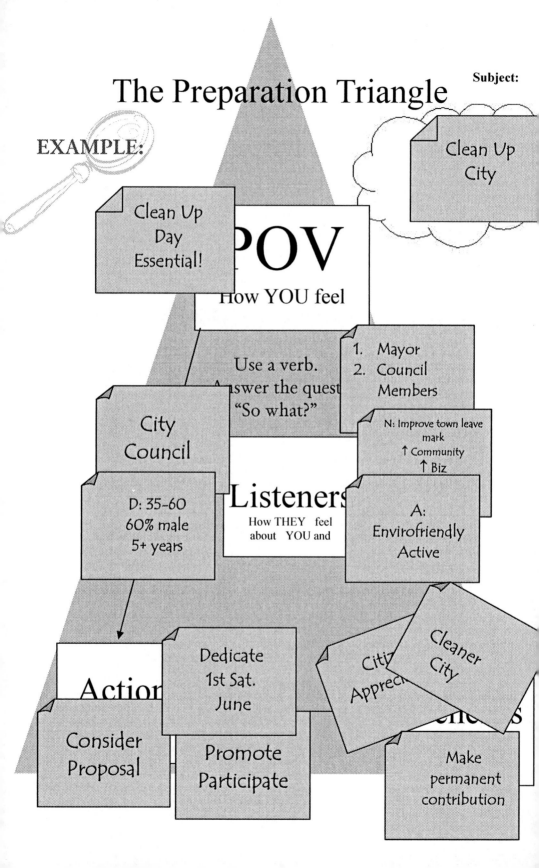

EXAMPLE:

Clean Up City

Clean Up Day Essential!

POV
How YOU feel

Use a verb.
Answer the question "So what?"

1. Mayor
2. Council Members

City Council

N: Improve town leave mark
↑ Community
↑ Biz

Listeners
How THEY feel about YOU and

D: 35-60
60% male
5+ years

A: Envirofriendly Active

Action

Dedicate 1st Sat. June

Citi Apprec

Cleaner City

Consider Proposal

Promote Participate

Make permanent contribution

The CREATE step is like doing a mental search and retrieval of anything that pops into your consciousness when you think of your subject. This is the time to brainstorm. Let your ideas flow in a rapid stream, uninterrupted by the tendency to prematurely organize. The result of a successful brainstorm is a deluge of facts, figures, stories, background, personal experiences, and case histories. New perceptions and ideas will occur to you during brainstorming that you would have missed in a more traditional process, such as writing from an outline.

It is essential to remember that order comes *after* chaos. This is the principal reason that The Decker Grid System is so effective. We are usually taught to create and organize at the same time. Our minds don't work that way.

Continuing with our city clean-up example, after reviewing my Cornerstones, I spent five minutes jotting down trigger words for every idea that came to me, using abbreviations and a personal shorthand to keep the words to a minimum. The results are as follows:

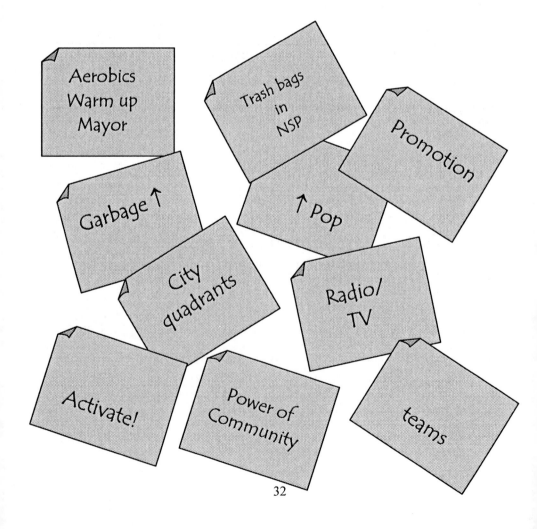

TO DO:

1 Set a timer for five minutes. Your objective is to brainstorm at least fifteen new ideas on Post-it Notes in this time.

2 Go! Write down any facts, ideas, concepts, details, case histories, examples, etc., that occur to you on your subject. Include stories, quotes and analogies. Do *not* censor!

3 Use trigger words or symbols.

4 Don't worry about putting the Post-It Notes in any kind of order. Avoid over-thinking or "wordsmithing."

5 Write quickly until time runs out!

KEY TO REMEMBER

- Set a time limit: Start with five minutes.

Cluster Like Crazy! The Cluster step creates order from your brainstorming. It is based on identifying the natural groupings that flow from the ideas you generated during the Create step. Clustering is the process of surveying your brainstorm results and identifying natural categories.

You now have ten to twenty randomly placed Post-it Notes from the **Create** step filling the surface in front of you. The object is to find the common themes.

When you have placed all of your ideas in clusters, the finapart of this step is to assign a label to each cluster. On another Post-it Note, write the title of the label and place it at the top of the cluster. The label should best capture the concept that the cluster addresses. Use trigger words for your labels and underline each one to distinguish it from the others in the cluster.

Your labels will become the **KEY POINTS** in your message. The Post-it Notes that make up each cluster become your SUB-POINTS. At this stage, you might have three to six clusters—each with anywhere from one to ten Sub-points within the cluster.

EXAMPLE:

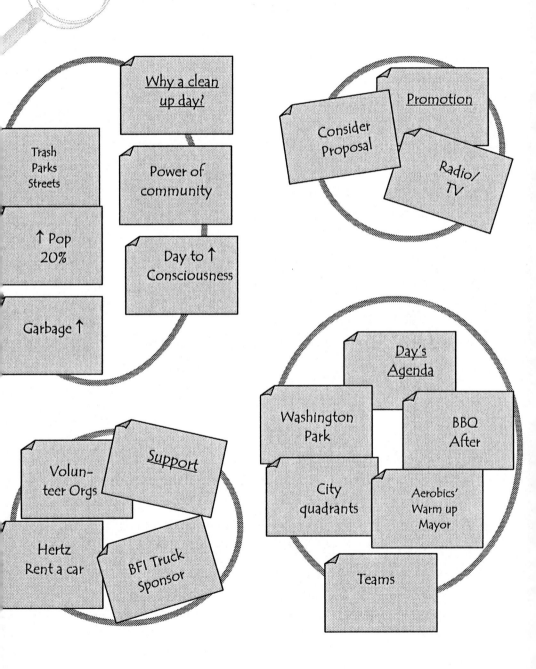

Why a clean up day?

Trash
Parks
Streets

↑ Pop 20%

Garbage ↑

Power of community

Day to ↑ Consciousness

Promotion

Consider Proposal

Radio/ TV

Support

Volun-teer Orgs

Hertz Rent a car

BFI Truck Sponsor

Day's Agenda

Washington Park

City quadrants

BBQ After

Aerobics' Warm up Mayor

Teams

TO DO:

1 Pick one Post-it Note (idea) and place it in the open space in front of you. Then find another idea that is similar to it and move it to that area. Add any other ideas common to that group to form a cluster.

2 Continue to move the Post-it Notes around to make clusters. They should be natural groupings that address or elaborate on the same point. Do not force all Post-it Notes into clusters.

3 When you have placed your ideas in clusters, assign a label or title to each cluster. Write the label on another Post-it Note, underline it, and place it at the top of the cluster.

4 Review each cluster and brainstorm for additional ideas. Review your Cornerstones to help stimulate your thinking. If ideas occur, capture them on Post-it Notes and add them to the appropriate cluster.

KEYS TO REMEMBER
- Group similar ideas together, creating clusters of two to ten Post-it Notes.
- Assign a label to describe each cluster, write it on a Post-it Note, and underline it. (Underlined labels become KEY POINTS, and the rest of the Post-it Notes within each cluster become SUB-POINTS.)
- Review each cluster and brainstorm for more ideas.

STEP 4

Compose Your Masterpiece. In the Compose step, you do the final organizing and editing of your ideas. You want to pare down to only your best ideas. You will compose the Body (the central part) of your message before you work on your Opening and Closing.

Begin with the Body. Keep it simple. People remember the main points, not every detail. Use the "Rule of Three": Have three key points, a proven standard of simplicity. This discipline will help you avoid a pitfall of many communicators, the dreaded "data dump." Dumping loads of information on hapless listeners is counterproductive since it tends to dilute, rather than strengthen, your impact.

On the right of your **Message Folder,** the layout provides places to put your three best Key Points at the top of each column. You'll move the best three Sub-points from the cluster under the corresponding Key Point.

When you're finished composing the Body, you will probably have several unused ideas on Post-it Notes. Review them to see if a **Key Point** from an unused cluster will make a better Sub-point than one already chosen. Rewrite to consolidate any overly detailed Post-it Notes.

EXAMPLE:

Looking back at the four clusters I've created, I will begin my work with *Why a clean up day?* Let's look at the cluster before and after I work through the Compose step.

KEY POINT ONE
BEFORE

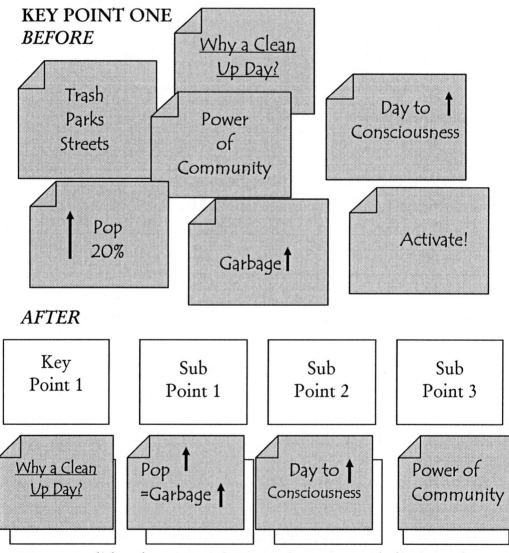

AFTER

I've consolidated two Post-it Notes into one and eliminated two altogether. Let's look now at Support and Promotion.

EXAMPLE:

In this case, I've combined two clusters into one and reworded Post-it Notes to make them more general. *BFI/Truck Sponsor* and *Hertz Rent-A-Car* were combined to become *Corp. Sponsors*. *Trash bags in NSP* and *Radio/TV* became one Post-it Note as well.

KEY POINT TWO

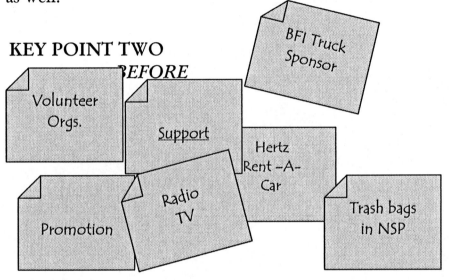

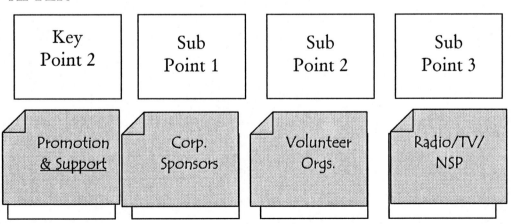

EXAMPLE:

The *BBQ After* and *Recycle Fair After* notes were combined and put as the last Sub-point because they will finish off the day. *Teams* and *City Quadrants* were combined. *Aerobics Warm-up by Mayor* will be used a little later in the section on Attention Getters and Memory Hooks.

KEY POINT THREE
BEFORE

Day's Agenda

BBQ After

City Quadrants

Teams

Washington Park Start-end

Aerobics Warm-up Mayor

Recycle Fair After

AFTER

Key Point 3	Sub Point 1	Sub Point 2	Sub Point 3

Day's Agenda

Kickoff Wash. Park

Teams/ Quadrants

BBQ/ Recyle Fair

TO DO:

1 With the Message Folder open, select the three most important Key Points (or labels) from your clusters. Prioritize them, placing the Post-it Notes in the appropriate Key Point boxes. Often your first Key Point will be introductory (the background or the current state) building to your third Key Point, the most important. Your sequence may be different; just arrange them for maximum impact.

2 Review all the Sub-points in your first Key Point. Cluster, pick the best three, and prioritize them. Place these ordered Sub-point Post-it Notes in the first column on the right side of your Message Folder.

3 Repeat the process in #2 for the remaining Key Points and selected Sub-points.

4 Look at your unused Post-it Notes to see if there are any that are better than the ones you've selected. Feel free to mix and match at this stage to capture all of your best ideas.

5 Do any rewriting that is necessary.

KEYS TO REMEMBER
- Compose the Body first.
- Remember the Rule of Three.
- Look for the best ideas and ways to consolidate multiple Post-it Notes into one.

Composing the Opening. There are many ways **to begin** your message. The basic Opening outlined here will serve as a standard for quick creativity and high effectiveness. It will provide a road map, letting your listeners know what benefits will result from taking the trip with you. You simply state your POV, General Action, and a summarized Benefit Statement. Later on, you will learn ways to add an effective **Attention Getter** in the Opening, but for now let's leave that space blank.

The beginning is the most important part of the work. —Plato

EXAMPLE:

4. COMPOSE

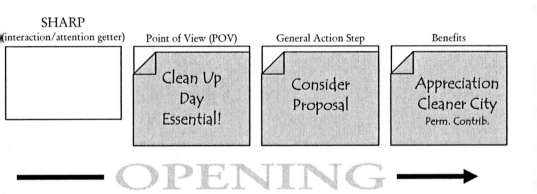

SHARP
(interaction/attention getter)

Point of View (POV)

Clean Up
Day
Essential!

General Action Step

Consider
Proposal

Benefits

Appreciation
Cleaner City
Perm. Contrib.

OPENING →

TO DO:

1   Return to the Cornerstones of the left side of your Message Folder. Most of the Post-it Notes from your Cornerstones will still be in place. If you used some in the Body of your message, re-create them for use in your Opening.

2   There is space for four Post-it Notes in the Opening section of the Message Folder. For now, leave the first Attention Getter box empty and place your POV Post-it Note next to it, as indicated. Your POV tells your listeners how you feel about your subject.

3   Place the General Action Post-it Note in the middle of the Opening panel. You will tell them what you want them to do in broad general terms.

4   Re-write your best benefits onto one Post-it Note. Place this Benefit Post-it Note on the right side of the Opening panel. You will complete your Opening by telling your listeners what's in it for them. By communicating the benefits right up front, you give your listeners a reason for listening.

KEYS TO REMEMBER

- A good opening is critical to setting the context for your message.
- State your POV.
- State your General Action Step.
- Give a summary of Benefits to listeners for taking your desired action.

Composing the Closing.

There are many ways to finish a message. The basic Closing outlined here is easy to create and effective when delivered. It will reinforce your ideas and commit you to leaving your listeners on a positive note. Later in the next section, we will add a Memory Hook to the closing; for now, let's just leave it blank.

You will simply restate your POV, tell your listeners the Specific Action(s) you want them to take (rather than the General Action used in the Opening), and leave your listeners by re-stating the Benefits they will receive from taking your desired actions.

As a final check, review your Listener Cornerstone, followed by POV, Actions, and Benefits. Then read over your Message Opening, Body, and Closing.

EXAMPLE:

I need to rewrite my POV and Benefit Post-it Notes to include in my Closing. I will take my Specific Actions and combine them on one Post-it Note for my Closing.

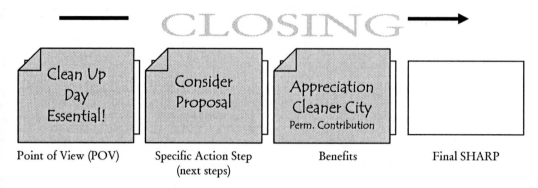

| Point of View (POV) | Specific Action Step (next steps) | Benefits | Final SHARP |

TO DO:

1 On a new Post-it Note, write the POV from your Opening, and place it on the left-most space of the Closing panel.

2 Returning to the Action Step Cornerstone from your Message Folder, place the Specific Action Steps in the middle of the Closing panel. (Whereas you will give your listeners the General Action Step in your Opening, giving them the Specific Actions in your Closing will sharpen their focus on exactly what you want them to do.) If you have more than one, consolidate them onto one Post-it Note.

3 On a new Post-it Note, write the summary of Benefits used in your Opening and place it on the right side of the Closing panel. Your last statement is your most memorable one. End your presentation by repeating the benefits to listeners of sharing your POV and taking your desired actions.

KEYS TO REMEMBER

It's time to review the final checklist and make adjustments. Have you:

- ❑ Stated your position and feeling (POV) on the subject?
- ❑ Addressed the needs and interests of your audience?
- ❑ Clearly communicated the actions you want your listeners to take within a certain time frame?
- ❑ Included the benefits they will receive by taking these actions?

If you answered no to any of these questions, you need to modify one or more Post-it Notes.

The Preparation Triangle

EXAMPLE:

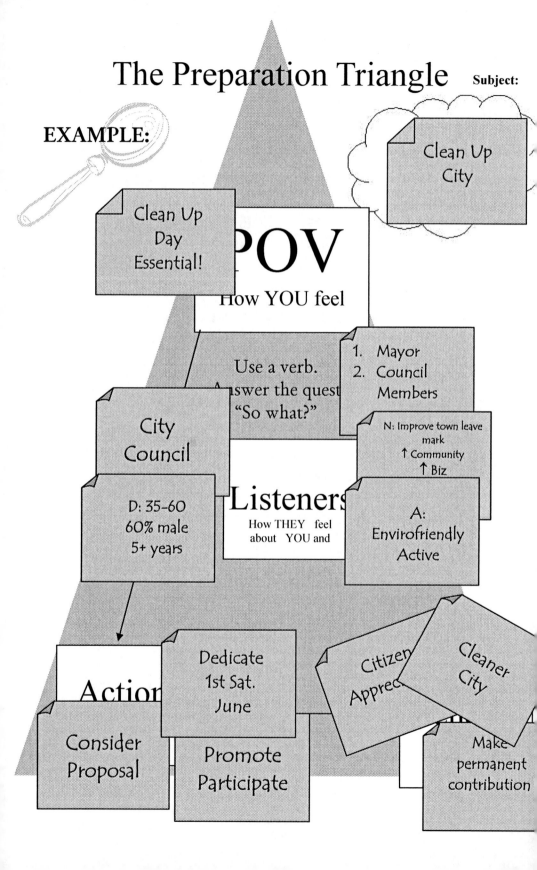

Clean Up City

Clean Up Day Essential!

POV
How YOU feel

Use a verb.
Answer the question
"So what?"

1. Mayor
2. Council Members

City Council

N: Improve town leave mark
↑ Community
↑ Biz

D: 35-60
60% male
5+ years

Listeners
How THEY feel about YOU and

A: Envirofriendly Active

Action

Dedicate 1st Sat. June

Citizen Apprec

Cleaner City

Consider Proposal

Promote Participate

Make permanent contribution

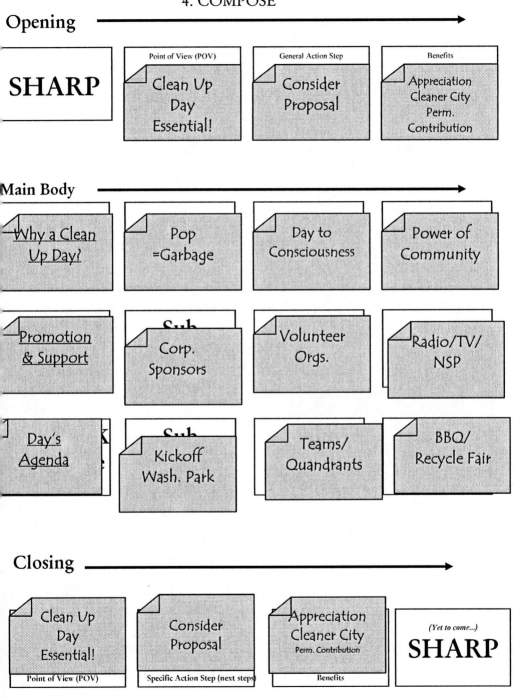

4. COMPOSE

Opening

SHARP	Point of View (POV)	General Action Step	Benefits
	Clean Up Day Essential!	Consider Proposal	Appreciation Cleaner City Perm. Contribution

Main Body

Why a Clean Up Day?	Pop =Garbage	Day to Consciousness	Power of Community
Promotion & Support	Sub Corp. Sponsors	Volunteer Orgs.	Radio/TV/ NSP
Day's Agenda	Sub Kickoff Wash. Park	Teams/ Quandrants	BBQ/ Recycle Fair

Closing

Clean Up Day Essential!	Consider Proposal	Appreciation Cleaner City Perm. Contribution	*(Yet to come...)* SHARP
Point of View (POV)	Specific Action Step (next steps)	Benefits	

49

SHARP!

ATTENTION GETTERS AND MEMORY HOOKS

Research has established that listeners remember the first and last comments made in a discussion or presentation better than the stuff in between. Therefore, it is critically important that you are effective in getting listener attention right away to increase the desire to pay attention to the body of your message. You must also provide a memorable closing statement that motivates them to take your desired action.

The key to obtaining and maintaining listener attention is the use of images and emotion created by language or visual support. The human mind loves images and emotion.

Why do people need help listening and remembering? Because they have a chronic case of information overload. That, coupled with an average adult attention span of eight seconds, means communicators have their work cut out for them!

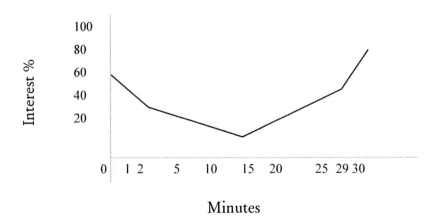

Minutes

Source: Effective Business and Technical Presentations, 3rd edition • George L. Morrisey & Thomas L. Sechrest

At Decker Communications, Inc. we have identified five principles that will enable you to capture audience attention, emphasize what is important in your information, and boost listener retention of your Key Points. We call them the SHARP principles:

S – Stories and Examples

H – Humor

A – Analogies

R – References and Quotes

P – Pictures/Visual Aids

Use these SHARP principles strategically and consciously in your communications. You need to identify one or two of these principles that work best for you naturally.

STORIES AND EXAMPLES

We all have personal experiences or know of others' experiences that can add humanity, depth, and emotion to our messages. Real-life experiences are the easiest to remember and use. Even hypothetical examples, allegories, and fairytales can be effective in making ideas more memorable.

Your story or example can be either directly or indirectly related, you'll need to work hard at making the link between it and your subject in the minds of your listeners by clearly stating the connection.

EXAMPLE:

Back to my Clean Up Day scenario, a story comes to mind about running in the park. A teenager in front of me opened a candy bar and threw the wrapper on the ground. I stopped, picked up the paper, handed it back to him and said, "The trash can is just over there." He proceeded to walk over and drop it in the can. He seemed to need that reminder. To remember my story, I will create the following Post-it Note:

Teenager
Candy

TO DO:

Take the time now to think about a story or example that would apply to your message. Use trigger words to write on a Post-it Note and put it to the side. You will add it to your grid later.

KEYS TO REMEMBER

- Be brief: 30 seconds to 1 minute maximum.
- Use sensory language to build word pictures in the minds of listeners.
- Tell the story as you would tell it sitting around the dinner table.
- After the story or example, state the point explicitly and relate it back to your POV or Key Point.

HUMOR

Incorporating humor into your message is not about telling jokes. Instead, it is about adding lightness and personality to your message.

Humor, properly used, helps bring energy to the people in the room and subconsciously reminds them of their uniquely human condition. The other big benefit of humor is that it helps to improve your delivery because it tends to increase your level of comfort and relaxation.

TO DO:

Take the time now to think about where you might add a little humor to your message. Write it down on a Post-it Note using trigger words and put it off to the side, next to your Story or Example.

EXAMPLE:

In my Clean Up Day example, I was thinking about the Kick-off in Washington Park and had an idea that made me smile. I could just picture the mayor leading an aerobics warm-up for all volunteers. If I can paint the word picture of the fun we could all have, it will add humor to my message. Here's my Post-it Note:

Mayor
Aerobic
Warm-up

KEYS TO REMEMBER

- Attitude: Let the lightness flow naturally.

- Don't be disappointed if your effort does not produce belly laughs. The intent is to add positive energy, not to be labeled a comedian.

- Balance humor with seriousness. Use humor strategically to draw attention to a particular point that is necessary to the core of your message.

- Exaggerate elements of your content to humorous proportions.

ANALOGIES

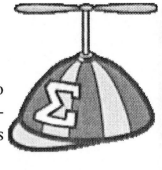

It is a natural function of the human mind to compare, contrast, categorize, and cross-reference. This function is what creates *analogies*.

To develop an analogy, ask yourself how your object, process, or concept is like something else. The similarities could be physical, emotional, or functional. Then write two or three trigger words on Post-it Notes to identify the analogy and put it off to the side, next to your Humor and Story Post-it Note.

Analogies not only help with listener interest and memory, they can also simplify a complex concept.

"Life is like a bowl of cherries" is a popular analogy.

EXAMPLE:

The concept of a community of people assembling for a Clean Up Day reminds me of the stories I've heard from my parents about a barn raising. They've told me of families coming from miles around to work from morning until night on getting a barn built and raised. I could talk about the power of bringing a community together to achieve a common goal using this barn raising analogy.

Barn
Raising

TO DO:

What analogy could you use in your message? Think of something similar to one of your Key Points or Sub-points and write it on a Post-it Note. Place it with the other SHARP Post-it Notes, which you will add to your message soon.

KEYS TO REMEMBER

- Use only one analogy per concept; otherwise, you diminish the effect.

- You must build the imagery around the link between the two ideas you are comparing. It is not enough to allude to things that have similarity. To be effective, you need to spend the time necessary to describe why and how the two items are similar.

- Vary the type of analogies you use. Don't just use analogies from sports or history. Be sensitive to your Listener Cornerstone in identifying analogous subjects that would make sense to your listeners based on their DNA.

- Choose analogies that have a positive emotional context.

REFERENCES AND QUOTES

A reference is any independent source of information that you cite to support your points. It can be something someone once did, an excerpt from an industry or trade journal, an article in a newspaper, or a program on radio or television.

A quote restates what someone else once said. It can be a formal quote from a book or article, an informal quote such a something your mother always said, a slogan that a company is using in an ad campaign, or lyrics from a song. Your local bookstore carries collections of quotations on various subjects. These books can be very handy when putting together your message that motivates.

EXAMPLE:

To support the increasing need for attention to a cleaner city, I would like to reference some statistics from City Hall on the increase in population of our city over the last few years and the resulting increase in trash. I called the garbage collection company and they provided some data on the increase in garbage trucks and tons of garbage going to the dump. In trigger words I create a Post-it Note as follows:

Stats on
pop. growth

TO DO:

Do you know of a quote that applies to your message? An article you read that was related to your topic? If so, add this Post-it Note to your collection of SHARP Post-it Notes.

KEYS TO REMEMBER...

Some helpful suggestions on using references and quotes:

- Read a quote rather than misquoting what someone said. Be sure to acknowledge the source if it is known.

- Introduce the reference or quote to prepare the listener(s) to pay close attention to what is coming.

- Select only the most powerful portions of a long reference or quote.

- Don't read lengthy passages.

- Don't leave this Attention Getter on its own. Instead, tie it back to your subject to ensure that its relevance is obvious.

The man who can think and does not know how to express what he thinks is at the level of him who cannot think.

—Pericles

PICTURES/VISUAL AIDS

A spoken message, reinforced with a well-designed visual aid, has greater impact than one merely spoken or communicated solely without the visual aid.

Pictures and visual aids are important in helping an audience understand a concept. Complex data can be organized and reduced to a graphic, a chart or a table to make a point clearly and concisely.

The most common problems with visual aids are: overuse, poor design and construction, and awkward transitions between the visual and the communicator.

THE FOLLOWING STATISTICS HELP TO COMMUNICATE THE POWER OF VISUAL SUPPORT:

- Retention increases from 14 to 38 percent when listeners see, as well as hear, a presentation.

- Presentations using visual aids were found to be 43 percent more persuasive than unaided presentations.

- Group consensus is 21 percent higher in meetings in which visual aids are incorporated.

- The time required to communicate a concept can be reduced up to 40 percent with the use of effective visuals.

Source: 3M Meeting Management Institute

The media you choose will help determine the look and feel of your visual. Your choice for any given communication event can also be effected by the following:

- Equipment/tools available
- Environment in which you will be communicating
- Number of listeners in the group
- Type of content to be represented visually

Software programs like Microsoft PowerPoint®, for designing and delivering visuals, have greatly increased the use of computer-based visuals in everything from one-on-ones to small meetings and presentations to hundreds. The benefits of computer-based visuals are the range of color and graphics available, the flexibility to make last-minute changes, the ability to put forth a professional image, and greater impact on listeners. Low-tech tools, such as flip charts and pads of paper, can still be highly effective tools for complementing a communicator.

Some of the best visual aids I have seen in my work with over 200,000 professionals have been props. A ball of yarn and scissors, an apple, a box wrapped with a big, beautiful red ribbon . . . These props are both simple and highly effective memory hooks for listeners. Be creative. Let your **imagination** run free!

EXAMPLE:

In my presentation to the City Council, I envision two opportunities for pictures/visual aids. The first one is for a dramatic opening in which I can show slides of the garbage that is now common in our parks and on our streets.

Also, in conjunction with the statistics on population and garbage growth, I can create a graph to help demonstrate the increases over the last five years.

Garbage
Pictures

Line Chart
Pop +
Garbage↑

TO DO:

What visual aids could you use to help communicate your concepts? Take a piece of paper and sketch some ideas about what your visuals might look like. Write two or three descriptive words on a Post-it Note and put it with your other SHARP Post-it Notes.

KEYS TO REMEMBER

When developing your visual aids, keep the three Bs in mind:

BIG – Make them large enough so that every listener can see them without squinting.

BOLD – Use bright, contrasting colors. Use pictures instead of words wherever possible.

BASIC – The goal is not to overwhelm, but to simplify the complex. If your visual is complicated it will detract from the effectiveness of your message.

ADDING IN YOUR ATTENTION GETTERS AND MEMORY HOOKS

TO DO:

It is now time to add the Attention Getters and Memory Hooks to your message. Open up your Message Folder and look at the SHARP Post-it Notes that you've created.

Which of them would help to get attention right away? Place this Post-it Note at the very beginning of your Opening.

Which of them would be most effective for powerfully reinforcing your message? This **Memory Hook** can become your final comment in your Closing.

The rest of your Attention Getters and Memory Hooks can be scattered sparingly throughout the body of your communication in places where they strategically complement a Key Point. Add the ones that will have the most impact. You can place them off to the side of your existing points, or replace a Sub-point with a SHARP if you feel it is more effective.

If you have some time between the preparation and delivery of your message, you may find even better SHARP examples that can be added and exchanged for your present ones.

EXAMPLE:

In evaluating the SHARP Post-it Notes I've generated for my Clean Up message, I have selected and arranged them as follows:

EXAMPLE:

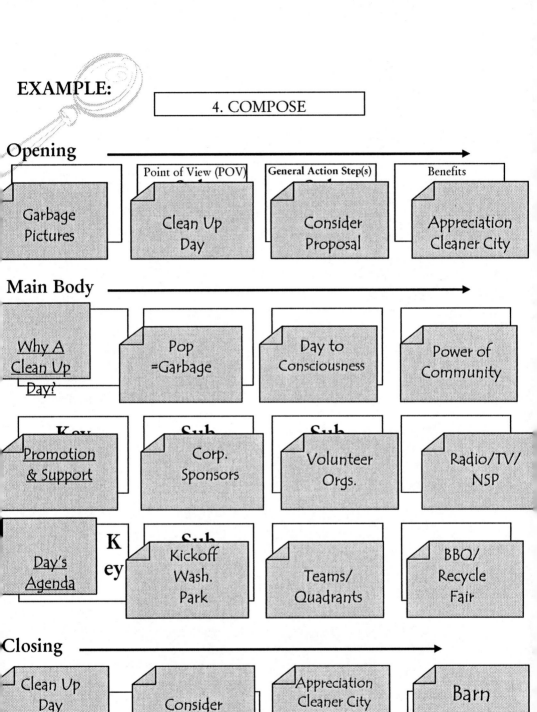

```
                    ┌─────────────────────┐
                    │     4. COMPOSE      │
                    └─────────────────────┘
```

Opening ──────────────────────────────►

	Point of View (POV)	General Action Step(s)	Benefits
Garbage Pictures	Clean Up Day	Consider Proposal	Appreciation Cleaner City

Main Body ──────────────────────────────►

Why A Clean Up Day?	Pop =Garbage	Day to Consciousness	Power of Community

Key...	Sub...	Sub...	
Promotion & Support	Corp. Sponsors	Volunteer Orgs.	Radio/TV/ NSP

Key	Sub...		
Day's Agenda	Kickoff Wash. Park	Teams/ Quadrants	BBQ/ Recycle Fair

Closing ──────────────────────────────►

Clean Up Day Essential!	Consider Proposal	Appreciation Cleaner City Perm. Contributions	Barn Raising
Point of View (POV)	Specific Action Step (next steps)		Final SHARP

67

STEP 5

Enough Preparation—Speak! Now that you have created a message that will motivate your listeners to take action, it is time to deliver it. The delivery of your message is critical to getting the results you want.

At my consulting firm, Decker Communications, we focus on individuals building the necessary skills to:

- Establish trust and believability
- Enhance their own natural communication style

We focus on these delivery skills to ensure a communicator's message is heard, understood, and acted upon.

- Sustaining eye communication to gain attention and build trust
- Maintaining strong posture and purposeful movement to communicate confidence and openness
- Using gestures and facial expressions to exude energy and attitude
- Using language and pauses to add clarity and emphasis
- Varying voice to radiate energy and emotion
- Ensuring appropriate dress and appearance to align with listeners
- Involving listeners to increase attention and retention
- Building on one's natural style to enhance trust and believability

If you feel that you can improve upon **how** you **communicate** your messages, take action. There are several ways to improve your skills. Seminars and private consultations are available from Decker Communications and others. There are also some excellent products available on the subject. We offer books, tapes and videos as tools. Practice and video feedback can be helpful. Take every **opportunity** to get **input** from others and to see yourself in action. Use this information to modify your communication behavior to make it more effective.

TA DA - YOU'RE ON!

It's time to communicate with your listeners. Deliver your message in the following sequence:

Opening – Start with your Attention Getter (SHARP). Transition to your POV. Then state General Action and Summary of Benefits.

Preview your Key Points – State the Key Points that you will discuss in the Body of your presentation. This previews the structure of your message and enables listeners to follow your "Table of Contents." Your preview may begin with the words, "Today I will discuss . . ."

Body -
> **Address Key Point #1** followed by its Sub-points
> **Address Key Point #2** followed by its Sub-points
> **Address Key Point #3** followed by its Sub-points

Do a Key Point Review – Summarize Key Points of the Body. It's important to review the Key Points to increase listener retention.

Closing – Communicate your POV, Specific Action Steps, and Benefit Summary along with your Memory Hook in the order that will have maximum listener impact.

Remember, above all else, the importance of making an emotional connection with your listeners. Speak genuinely and from the heart and you'll go a long way toward being most effective whenever you communicate.

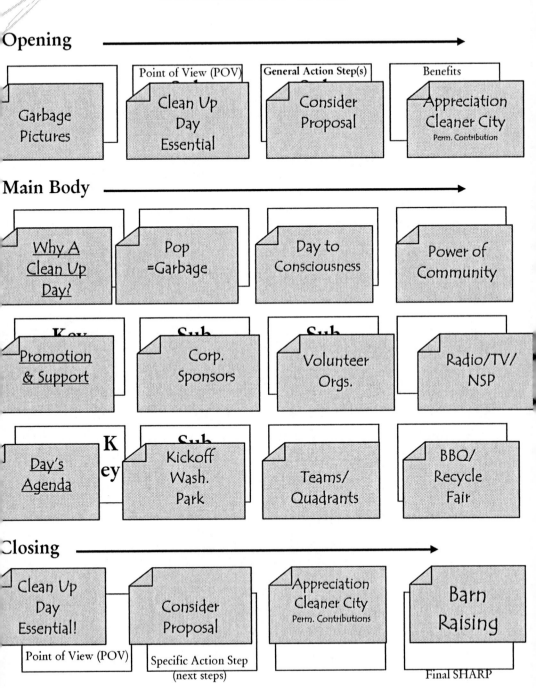

COMPLETE GRID

EXAMPLE:

Opening

| Garbage Pictures | Point of View (POV) — Clean Up Day Essential | General Action Step(s) — Consider Proposal | Benefits — Appreciation Cleaner City Perm. Contribution |

Main Body

| Why A Clean Up Day? | Pop =Garbage | Day to Consciousness | Power of Community |

| Promotion & Support | Corp. Sponsors | Volunteer Orgs. | Radio/TV/ NSP |

| Day's Agenda | Kickoff Wash. Park | Teams/ Quadrants | BBQ/ Recycle Fair |

Closing

| Clean Up Day Essential! | Consider Proposal | Appreciation Cleaner City Perm. Contributions | Barn Raising |

Point of View (POV) — Specific Action Step (next steps) — Final SHARP

71

APPLICATION 1:
TIME FOR A QUICKIE!

When you have just five minutes to prepare, use the Quick Grid. For most of us, ample preparation time is a luxury we can rarely afford. When you have just minutes to prepare for a meeting or discussion, use the Quick Grid.

The Quick Grid streamlines the Create and Compose steps, thereby saving some time in preparation. To use the Quick Grid, lay the Cornerstones as usual. Then, instead of doing creative brainstorming for five minutes, simply write down the first three Key Points that come to mind. Put them in order of chronology or importance, with the most important last.

Now brainstorm quickly on each Key Point to generate two or three Sub-points to support it.

You have now created the Body of your message in two to three minutes with Cornerstones to use in your Opening and Closing. If everyone in the group or meeting has had little time to prepare, your ability to generate a **Quick Grid** will help you shine. Try it. We know you'll see a difference.

KEYS TO REMEMBER
- Identify Subject and lay your Cornerstones.
- Write down the first three Key Points that come to mind.
- Quickly brainstorm each Key Point for one to three Sub-points.
- Move Cornerstones to opening and rewrite them for Closing.

APPLICATION 2:
INCREASING YOUR PHONE POWER

People are often least effective at communicating messages that motivate listeners when they're using the telephone.

When you call someone, do you take the moment necessary to establish the context (Cornerstones), collect your thoughts, and identify your Key Points? If you don't, you should. It will be the difference between rambling and communicating a net, action-oriented message.

If you use The Decker Grid System to create your message, you will be perceived as professional and credible. So what are you waiting for? Now that you have walked yourself through the process, use it to prepare for your next phone conversation.

The Decker Grid System works whether you're communicating with someone live on the phone or through a voicemail message. It works for both outgoing and incoming calls. If someone calls you, spend a few seconds at the beginning of the call identifying your Cornerstones on the subject being discussed.

APPLICATION 3:
MAXIMIZING YOUR MEETING EFFECTIVENESS

Most of us spend far too much time in meetings. There are few things worse than sitting in an unproductive meeting, privately agonizing over the piles of work awaiting your return. Don't contribute to meeting mindlessness. Be a role model. Startle your associates by becoming a productive meeting contributor.

If you are the host of the meeting, use the Grid format to construct the actual agenda—from your POV for holding the meeting, to the actions you want your attendees to take, and the benefits to them. Your agenda items should be created from your Key Points.

If you are presenting a particular item on the agenda and you have some advance notice, prepare your complete message using the Grid format.

If you are called upon in a meeting without advance warning, ask for a moment to collect your thoughts and lay the Cornerstones of your message in your mind or on the paper in front of you.

Talkers have **ALWAYS** ruled. They will continue to rule. The smart thing is to join them. —Bruce Barton

KEYS TO REMEMBER

- Begin with how you feel about the subject being introduced (POV).
- Ask yourself how the rest of the people in this meeting feel about the subject and your Point of View. What is their DNA? (Listener Cornerstone)
- What action do you want them to take to support your Point of View? (Action Steps)
- What benefits will there be for the people in attendance if they do as you suggest? (WIIFM—"What's in it for me?")

Simply by laying the Cornerstones, you will be able to articulate a concise, action-oriented message that will impress your fellow meeting attendees. And you'll be more likely to get the results you want. That's how powerful this simple tool can be!

APPLICATION 4:
CREATING PRESENTATIONS THAT PRODUCE RESULTS

Your ability to inspire your listeners to take **your desired action** is the key to your success. Formal presentations are usually high-stakes situations in which you have much riding on the buy-in of your listeners. Don't waste this precious opportunity by communicating a less-than-powerful message.

You can't afford to be less than crystal clear. You must have punch and pizzazz and communicate a sincere **Point of View**. The last thing you want is for your listeners to be tuning out or thinking, *What is the point here?*

Formal presentations still involve one person communicating ideas persuasively to others. The **key** ingredients of The Decker Grid System are as critical in this presentation format as in any other. In fact, in a high-stakes presentation, there is even more riding on your ability to impress, inform, and inspire your listeners to take action.

SOME HELPFUL HINTS IN MAXIMIZING YOUR PRESENTATION TIME

1 Use the 75 percent rule. Practice your presentation using only 75 percent of your actual allotted time. Why? Because, invariably, in a real situation with questions, improvisations, and extrapolations, you'll end up using more time than you did during your practice session. If your total rehearsal time is fifteen minutes, your actual presentation will run about twenty minutes.

2 Feel free to reference your notes. You should not memorize every Post-it Note, nor should you hold your Message Folder in your hand. Simply place it nearby and, if necessary, pause, walk over to your notes, read the trigger words for the next section, move back to your speaking position, and begin speaking. Presenters are often uncomfortable with these silences; listeners, however, are not. It seems perfectly natural to watch someone pause to collect his or her thoughts. Try it and see!

3 Build in opportunities to involve your audience so that the communication is not all one-way. There are many ways to engage listeners, including asking questions, soliciting comments, and having listeners participate in exploring solutions with you.

4 Include Attention Getters and Memory Hooks, especially in your Opening and Closing. They can also be placed strategically in support of your Key Points. They may include one or more of the SHARP principles.

APPLICATION 5:
HOSTING A SUCCESSFUL ALL-DAY MEETING OR SEMINAR

The Decker Grid System is enormously effective in developing agendas for one- or two-day meetings.

To develop and deliver a full-day communication event, follow these steps:

1 Develop your first Grid for the entire event. Carry out all of the steps including laying the Cornerstones, Creating, Clustering, and Composing.

2 Evaluate your Key Points: Determine whether they should become actual modules or sections in your meeting or seminar. Then create a Grid based on that Key Point as the Grid subject.

3 When you lay the Cornerstones for this module, base it specifically on your POV, Listeners, Action Steps, and Benefits for the Key Point in question and not for the entire day-long program.

4 Continue this process for each of your Key Points.

Once completed, you should have an overall Grid that maps out the entire day, and one Grid for each Key Point, or section of the day.

By using The Decker Grid System to develop and deliver your all-day event, you will ensure that your participants receive a format that is listener-based and action-oriented. The information will be relevant to them and delivered in an interesting way that makes sense.

INTERACTING WITH YOUR VISUALS

One of the biggest mistakes communicators make is failing to *introduce* their visual support. Be sure to tell the audience what they are about to see.

It is also critical to *pause* when displaying and then changing each visual. Listeners need at least a few seconds to orient themselves toward the new stimuli. If there are words on the visual, they need the time to read them before you begin speaking. And *don't read* the visuals to the audience.

We highly recommend building in blanks between your visuals to give you the time to re-focus the listeners on you, the communicator. Using PowerPoint®, you can simply hit the "B" key on your keyboard to make the screen blank (many remotes also provide a "blackout" feature).

Using Attention Getters and Memory hooks effectively can make the difference between being a good communicator and an outstanding one. The Stories, Humor, Analogies, References/quotes, and Pictures/visual aids you use help ensure that your listeners have an interesting and informative experience when you communicate with them. By incorporating SHARPs into your message, you make it easier for your listeners to tune in and stay with you. You enhance the probability that they will remember the key elements of your message and will be inspired to take your desired action.

USE IT OR LOSE IT

Taking skills from practice to application is the most challenging and rewarding part of the learning process. Make the commitment to yourself that the very next message you communicate will benefit from the enormous power of The New Decker Grid System. Whether it is a phone conversation, an agenda item at a meeting, or an hour-long presentation, your message will motivate your listeners to take action because it will contain all of the necessary ingredients for success. Those are:

FOUR CORNERSTONES TO SET THE CONTEXT

- Clear **Point of View** on your subject
- A message that is focused on your **Listeners**
- Clear, realistic, and measurable **Action Steps**
- **Benefits** to listeners for taking those actions

STRUCTURE TO HELP LISTENERS FOLLOW WHAT YOU ARE SAYING

- Three Key Points that are previewed, stated, and repeated
- Three Sub-points that give depth to each Key Point
- A powerful Opening and Closing to frame the Body of your message

ELEMENTS THAT ADD INTEREST AND HEART TO YOUR MESSAGE

Attention Getters and Memory Hooks to boost listening and retention and connect you emotionally with your listeners. These are the SHARPs (Stories and Examples, Humor, Analogies, References and Quotes, and Pictures/Visual Aids).

We encourage you to accept the challenge of communicating memorable messages that motivate others to take action and get results. The Decker Grid System will go a long way in getting you there as long as you use it and persevere.

For questions on The Decker Grid System or any other Decker Communications services, please call (415) 752-0700 or visit our web site: DeckerMethod.com.

Thank you for your interest—and good communicating!

Bert Decker

About the Author

Bert Decker has appeared many times on NBC's *Today Show* as their communications expert, often commenting on the U.S. presidential debates, as well as ABC's *20/20* and other national media. He is the author of the best-selling book, *You've Got To Be Believed To Be Heard,* and *Communicating With Bold Assurance,* as well as several other books, video and audio programs. Bert personally coaches CEOs, such as Charles Schwab, major sports figures like Olympic Gold Medal–winners Bonnie Blair and Tom Dolan, NFL All-Pro tight end Brent Jones, and politicians, such as Representative Nancy Pelosi, the first woman in American history to be majority leader of the House of Representatives.

In 1979, Bert founded Decker Communications, Inc., an executive development company specializing in coaching executives and leaders in communications. The methodology is based on his discoveries and experiences of the last 25 years in communication and leadership. The company is now considered to be the leading communications training firm in the United States. Bert's philosophy was and continues to be that there is no one way to communicate—every person has a natural style. That principle is at the heart of The Decker Method and is the reason there are over 200,000 confident graduates of the company's core programs.

Bert also founded Vision Videos, a film and video production company. His company creates films and videos that utilize the advantages of today's Digital Video technology to leverage persuasive communications for corporations, nonprofits and individuals. He recently created the award-winning film, *Behind The Shield* for The Salvation Army.

Bert personally consults on vision, leadership, communications and seminars that sell. He continues to speak, write and direct on making an impact in the marketplace, and coaches executives and leaders with the Decker Platinum Executive Coaching Program, and other programs.

Resources To Help You Master
What You've Just Read

You've Got to Be Believed to Be Heard: Reach the First Brain to Communicate in Business and in Life (Book, $15) Best-selling business book on the behavior that counts to make an impact.

> "This is a breakthrough book, with new important ideas. After reading it you will be a believer ... that success and fulfillment are achievable only if you're an effective communicator. And it shows the way."
> —W. Pendleton Tudor, Chairman, *AdWeek*

Effective Communication Skills (DVD, $29)
One-hour video seminar of Bert Decker with principles for personal impact and the essential behavioral skills.

> "Bert Decker is to communicating what Tom Peters is to management."
> —Judith Briles, Author, *The Confidence Factor*

Creating Focused Messages . . . Every Time (DVD, $29)
One-hour video seminar of Bert Decker demonstrating the four steps of The Decker Grid so you can create a focused, listener-based message every time.

> "The Decker Method is a must for anyone who wants to succeed."
> —Charles Schwab

Order these and other resources, including Message Folders, by calling (415) 752-0700.

Decker Communications, Inc. also provides **public and customized training programs** to **enhance communications and leadership skills,** which include:

Communicate to Influence

A two-day small group program (limited to 12) with extensive video feedback and private coaching. Teaches the nine behavioral skills and using The Decker Grid to create focused listener based messages.

Communicating for Leadership

A one-day interactive program for larger groups teaching the principles of communication for leaders and managers, including the Decker methodology for personal impact and the Decker Grid.

Platinum Executive Communication Coaching

A personal, one-on-one coaching session with Bert Decker, one day with follow-up, includes extensive video feedback and continuous personal coaching, focusing on the executive's specific needs.

For more information, or to order Message Folders, call (415) 752-0700.

Decker Communications, Inc.
104 Point Lobos
San Francisco, CA 94121

info@DeckerMethod.com

DeckerMethod.com